The Shape of the Tree

The Shape of the Tree

SELECTED POEMS

John Janeway Conger

EQUINOX MOUNTAIN PRESS   DENVER, COLORADO

Thanks to the following publications in which some of these
poems first appeared: *The Colorado Quarterly, Touchstone*
(Amherst College), and *The Asheville School Review.*

All inquiries and permission requests should be addressed to the
publisher, Equinox Mountain Press, 950 South Cherry Street,
Suite 718, Denver, Colorado 80222.

First Edition

Printed in the United States of America
Library of Congress Catalog Card Number: 93-7036
ISBN 0-9635839-0-5

FOR TRISTA

CONTENTS

AUTHOR'S NOTE

The poems selected for this collection were written between 1943 and 1992, most of them in recent years. In general, the poems are presented in reverse chronological order, beginning with my most recent poem and ending with a poem about poetry itself—and love—written at sea in the middle of World War II.

J.J.C.

Landgrove, Vermont
October 3, 1992

AUTUMN

Walking downhill in the morning mist
Past ghosts of yellow and red,
The old man could only see clearly
The road that lay just ahead.

All of the roads he had taken,
The hills that he used to climb,
Seemed lost, like the dreams of childhood,
Somewhere in the mists of time.

Then suddenly the sun burned through,
And he saw in the autumn air
The circling hills and the town below,
And the shape of his life, laid bare.

SUGAR MAPLE

Even when you were young,
No taller than a five-year-old,
Your leaves were always the first to turn,
Copper and red and gold,

As though somehow you knew
A secret others could not sense
(A quickening in the wind?) foretelling
Winter's reticence.

Though you have grown about
As tall as sugar maples grow,
You still acknowledge autumn first,
And the promise of cold and snow,

As if to tell the world
You do not fear the seasons,
That spring and summer, fall, and even
Winter have their reasons.

MERRY-GO-ROUND

In the long afternoon
The merry children
Went round and round
Hoping to catch the brass ring,
But not really caring:
The calliope's insistence
And the prancing of the painted horses
Held promises enough.

In the lengthening shadows
Of the long afternoon
The children heard the sound of distant trumpets
And spurred their horses on,
Dreaming of castles rising in the mist
In another country
Somewhere at the end of time.

ABOVE TIMBERLINE

If it had grown in ampler soil,
Not clinging to chinks in stone,
On kinder slopes with other trees,
Not windswept and alone,

It would have grown straight and even,
Not sculpted by wind and rain —
Stretched like the curl of an incoming wave
Seeking the shore again.

The shape it bears is its alone,
And still, for all its scars,
On moonless nights we see that it
Lives closer to the stars.

SIX DAYS OUT

In the deep swells and silence of the sea,
The sounds of water lapping on the hull
And the luffing of the sails in errant air
Yield only to the crying of a gull.

While earth and heaven meet in darker blue
No cloud disturbs a perfect symmetry:
The constant circle of the changing sea
Is all the world for this small boat and me.

REPORT CARD

(In memory of Pfc. Lynn Richardson Pitcher, age 21,
Landgrove Village, Vermont. Killed in the Battle of the
Bulge, World War II, Saurlauten, Germany, 1945.)

If you were to return to this village
You would know at once that you were home.

Now, there's a modest monument beside the road
Across from where you lived: a bright new flag
Above an upturned stone that bears the names
Of five who lost to war their unfilled dreams—
Five from a village of three hundred souls!

Everything else is pretty much the same:

Some childhood trees reach closer to the sky;
A few have fallen from old age or blight,
And in their shadows others have sprung up
To take their place: maple, oak, and birch.

Many of the people that you knew are gone:
The parents of the friends who shared your dreams;
Some of your friends, too, have long since left,
But some have stayed, and others have returned
To claim again in age the land they love.

As for the rest, the houses and the barns,
The open meadows and the closing trees,
The small white church, the churchyard, and the school,
The sun-stirred, dusty road that links them all,
The bouldered stream below the bridge,
In which you fished and swam in icy pools,
Laughing—in love with life, and girls, and art:

All are as you left them, as though waiting
Changeless in a world of constant change
Through all the years of summer, fall, and winter,
And yet another spring, for your return
To apple blossoms white with wonder, and
Wild flowers burst upon the greening hills.

If you were to return, would you be sad
For what has changed, or glad for what has not?

TRANSITION

In the summer stillness
We lie together on a green hill,
Dreaming that time has stopped;
Only sunlight stirs the dust.

Suddenly a cold wind rises,
Sending a shiver through the grass.
Night will come early;
In the morning there will be frost.

OLYMPIC SKATER

I do not know why it should strike me so,
But there was something in her willow grace—
This tiny figure like a humming bird,
Pausing a moment motionless, her face

All sunlight in the caverned hall, then gone
Like a remembered dream, a flash of steel
Carving perfection in the hard, reluctant ice
With soaring gull-like turns—that made me feel,

If only for a moment, that the ghosts
Of starless nights and the long winter's death
Were exorcized, like sleep-imprisoned youth
Wakened to morning by a lover's breath.

Perhaps because she seemed so much alone—
A solitary lark that seeks the sky—
No more could those who dwell in shadows sigh
That grace and courage only live to die.

REMEMBRANCE

Returning late to hills that once were home,
Just as the rain began before the night,
I watched the apple trees of childhood fade
As woods and meadow merged in silver light.

Was this the place so many seasons gone
Where laughter ringed the hills, and love was born
Like new bright leaves unfolding in the sun,
Renewing ancient trees by winter worn?

II

Along the misty, rutted roads of time
I came upon a sudden shaft of light,
Etching in gold lost dreams we once had dreamed;
But then the dark closed in, and they took flight.

THE SEA

Time loses its way
Among the hills and valleys
Of the sea.

THOSE THINGS ARE LOVELIEST

Those things are loveliest we cannot keep:
Windsong at evening on a still-warm hill,
Or sudden stars seen through a gathering mist—
The whispered breath of love when all is still.

Those things are truest that we cannot see:
The ghosts of childhood in a world apart,
Seas we have journeyed only in a dream—
The inward vision of a searching heart.

THE HILL

Copper and gold and sudden red,
The leaves of summer fall;
Naked against a cold blue sky,
An ancient birch stands tall.

The old man has come home at last
For dreams he once knew there,
Only to find the autumn winds
Have stripped its branches bare:

But still he draws himself erect
And starts back down the hill,
Protected only by his pride
Against the evening chill.

FOR TASHY

(In memory of Natasha Congdon, 1961–1978)

Because there was so much of these in you,
Of sunlight laughing on a mountain stream,
The freshening breeze that comes to meet the dawn,
Stars seen through a gathering mist, as in a dream . . .

Because there was so much of these in you,
Of earth still warm after the sun has set,
Wild-flowered hills in spring, but most of all,
Life to be lived as whole without regret,

And carefree love because you cared so much,
Each stirs a sadness now time does not ease,
But each becomes more precious and more true,
Because there is so much of you in these.

SILENCES

Silent as snow,
As stars,
As misty seas,

They sat before the fire
Long into the night,
Their love unspoken in the shadowed lights,

But limitless as falling snow,
As true as stars,
As deep as misty seas.

METROPOLIS

There is no comfort here:
The heart too long alone
That seeks for velvet warmth
Meets only steel and stone.

There is no beauty here:
Deprived of earth and sky,
The soul can only feed
Upon itself or die.

THE SHAPE OF THE TREE

The maple's leaves turn quickly now,
Bright orange, red, and gold;
No longer do the warm mists rise
To meet the morning cold.

As randomly in windless air
The leaves begin to fall,
Summer seems lost in a waking dream
Almost beyond recall.

Although the days grow shorter, still
The heart must not despair;
Only when the last leaf falls
Is the shape of the tree laid bare.

THE HOUR WAS LATE

The hour was late and the shortest way
From the upland fields to the farm
Was through a darkened stretch of wood
Where a snapped twig spreads alarm.

The wood was thick with underbrush
And the ghosts of fallen trees;
Time seemed to stop until my eyes
Could mark their shapes with ease.

Then suddenly, as sunlight breaks
Through a rent in leaden skies,
I saw a forgotten glade ahead,
And heard the careless cries

Of a girl and boy who had come upon
This island as their own,
Where there was space to laugh and dream
Together—and alone.

I would have liked to join them there,
Squinting against the sun,
Briefly to shed the cold and damp
Before my walk was done.

But I could not breach the sunlit space
That now was all their pride.
I saw the shadows lengthening
Like an incoming evening tide

And knew in the dark of a fading dream
That late had been so bright,
They soon might need the help of eyes
Familiar with the night.

SONG FOR MY MOTHER

It is now a month that you are gone—
A month since all the dying and the pain
Of winter's sad decline that kept from me
The memories that let you live again

As you once were. But now the snows are past.
The sleeping earth awakes to warm spring rain,
A fragile leaf unfurls, a new bird sings,
And I can see you clearly once again:

A young wife standing on a grassy dune,
Laughing, the seawind fresh upon your face,
As I played tag with the ocean's ebb and flow,
Tumbling through waves that I could not outrace.

Years later when in war I went to sea,
I never felt the fear that others knew;
The perils of the sea were real enough,
But somehow I felt safe because of you.

Two men you loved the most and who loved you
Died young—your father when you were twelve and then
My own at fifty-nine. What could have turned
From grief to bitterness became again

The love you shared—in which our children grew.
And they sensed, too, the adventurous child who hid
Behind the patient caring when they said:
"Promise that you'll always stay a kid!"

So many years you rose most days alone
And had your morning coffee while you read
The *Journal* and *The New York Times*. You did
Not passively accept the world; instead

Injustice and pretense were met with scorn,
Caring with joy. At times you would surprise,
If not alarm, your broker with the news
Zambian copper warrants were "bound to rise."

Your mother's fortune crumbled in your youth,
But you received far greater gifts from her:
An inner wellspring to survive the drought
Of loneliness; and knowing who you were.

You wore your courage lightly and with grace.
No longer will your restless spirit roam:
Now after all the pain, you are with those
Whom you loved first. I hope you are at home.

SONNET

Shyly at first, the snow begins to fall,
Lighter than air, as intricate as lace:
Now on a naked branch, a rock, this wall,
Its beggars' jewels are strewn with random grace.
Then grown in confidence, veil upon veil,
It casts its endless whiteness on the air:
The farthest hills recede, the town turns pale,
And I am left alone in silence. Where?

While my world shrinks, the universe expands
Beyond man's hope of heaven. Still there are,
Outside the stillness, eyes and ears and hands
That strain to catch the pulsing of a star.
While some must reach as far as they can see,
This silent space is world enough for me.

NIGHT RAIN

At night's remotest hour,
Just before the dawn,
I lie in my bed
In a land unknown
Wondering where time has gone.

All sound has long departed,
The last bird taken flight;
Darkness is all
Where the silence
Echoes against the night.

Suddenly there is the whisper
Of rain on roof and stone,
The sky grows light,
A lone bird calls:
I am no longer alone.

ASPEN

Twelve aspen leaves lay scattered
In careful disarray
Across a field of velvet green,
Each perfect in its way.

No two alike, the jeweller said,
Since each was veined by God,
Its prodigal asymmetry
In finest silver shod.

No less themselves than these are men,
Who blindly seek to see
And draw their lives in blood to buy
Brief immortality,

While golden aspen cast their leaves
To wind, and snow, and rain
In quiet, timeless confidence
That spring will come again.

THE CHILDREN

Quietly as gentle winds on water,
Softly as the fast-approaching night,
He speaks, and yet is heard above the thunder
Of the self-appointed oracles of Right.

While we diagram the boundaries of heaven
And adjust our minor differences with lead,
He whispers down the winter winds of morning,
"But the children . . . my children, are they fed?"

We are disturbed in minor ways to hear him
Invading thus our many-sided fate:
"To simplify is never hard," we murmer,
"And the problems that we face, of course, are great;

And even if the issues all were clearer,
So few cannot do much and are not free."
Even thus it seemed to him who once was bidden,
"Give to the poor and come and follow me."

ON EARTH, PEACE

I have walked at evening
Alone in the silence of snow
Where sudden trees, like gentle ghosts,
Nod gravely as I go.

I have waked to morning
On mountains laughing with light
And watched the restless fields below
Throw back the quilts of night.

Where secret worlds lie breathless,
Blue-green beneath the sea,
I have sought through pulsing grasses
The bright anemone.

Now darker nights surround me
And the farthest sun has set;
To come once more to such as these
Would be enough, and yet

The many roads I've travelled,
Sun-stirred or etched with rain,
The roads that are what I've become
I shall not know again

Till peace shall come like April rain
To desert, plain, and hill,
And the meadow lark is heard again,
And the shattered air is still.

VERMONT GRAVEYARD

There is so much of stillness here:
The secret leaf, the silent stone . . .
Only the grass that rustles near
To tell me I am not alone.

HUMMING BIRD

I wonder if the humming bird
That darts from flower to flower
Ever finds a resting place
Before its final hour.

I wonder if the man whose life
Is not built stone on stone
With pain the mortar of his joy
Will find his soul a home.

HOMECOMING

I have come back to these:
To fields my father mowed
Year after quiet year,
To apple blossoms newly born,
Pink-shy and tentative,
And trembling in the morning air;
To water laughing down a hill
Where we once, laughing too,
Tumbled and splashed from rock to rock,
Happy in the timelessness of youth.

I have come back at last to these—
Such strands of hope as now remain,
Suspended in a paradox:
Can leaf and blossom,
Water, earth, and air
(Those elements that seasons seek to tame)
Be ever changing, yet remain the same?

METAMORPHOSIS

The fragile leaf that first unfurls
With shy and proper mien,
And, trembling, seeks the April sun
Is dressed in palest green.

But fed by summer sun and rain,
And stirred by winds unseen,
It gains the confidence to don
A coat of deeper green.

Only when the nights grow long
And the sap has ceased to flow
Does it defer to death, and fall
Blood-red against the snow.

WARTIME CHRISTMAS, 1945

The silent snows have come to hide
The rutted fields from view;
The withered grasses, sleeping now,
In spring will rise anew.

But there can be no snows to hide
The death of faceless men
Who never will rise up from sleep
To plant and sow again.

ÉTUDE IN DOUBT MAJOR

Sitting again as I have sat before,
Uncertainly aware of certain facts—
A dim reality of white, a door
Too large upon the eye, forgotten acts
Of emptiness that rise to cloud the brain,
A shadow on my paper, and the sound
Of far-off voices like the too full rain,
Where winter's dying memories are found:

I am become too conscious, as the man
Too conscious is become that grasps his chair
With hot, wet hands, and grasping, never can
Erase some shriek of dying from the air;
All knowledge by one echo pressed away,
Each nerve-end aches with nothing left to say.

CANDLELIGHT QUATRAIN

Softly my candle burns,
The clear wax meets the cold,
The flame flares bright in an endless night . . .
How soon the new is old!

POETRY

Somewhere
Always
Between the overwhelming fact of existence
And the precise fact of expression,
Between the formless being
And the well-shaped saying,
Between the pain
And the recollection,
The loving and the remembrance—
Always
Somewhere
The breathing stops.

And yet I do not find it strange:
Knowing a poem only is,
And never can
Become,
Knowing the stuff of poetry
Is wordless
As grief is wordless;
Formless
As love is
As hope
As time is.

Knowing so much
Yet profiting withal
So little:
Because I love you,
Because I still try,
Quietly
With the softness of starlight on water,
Hopelessly
With the anger of rain on windows,
To penetrate the emptiness of words,

Only to find
The wind gone cold again,
The starlight set,
The ash gone white . . .

But I do love you!

About the Author

JOHN JANEWAY CONGER lives in Colorado, where he is professor emeritus at the University of Colorado. He was born in 1921 in New Brunswick, N.J., and grew up there and in southern Vermont, where he still spends part of each year. He began writing and publishing poetry while still a student, first at The Asheville School in North Carolina, and then at Amherst College, where he was encouraged by the poet David Morton. After service in the Navy in World War II, where he commanded a destroyer escort in the Atlantic Fleet, Conger obtained a Ph.D. in psychology at Yale University. Over more than forty years as a teacher, clinician, researcher, academic administrator, foundation officer, and government advisor, his greatest interest has been the well-being of the Nation's children and youth. He is the author or coauthor of more than a dozen books on child and adolescent development, which have been translated into a like number of languages around the world. And he has been active throughout his career in advocating greater recognition of the needs of children, adolescents, and families in our society. In 1987, he received the American Psychological Association's lifetime Award for Distinguished Contributions to Psychology in the Public Interest. This is his first book of poetry.